CHRISTMAS IN OUR HEARTS

Christmas In Our Hearts

by CHARLES L. ALLEN
and CHARLES L. WALLIS

FLEMING H. REVELL COMPANY

Acknowledgment is made to the following, who have granted permission for the reprinting of copyrighted material:

Abingdon Press for story from *The Village Tragedy* by Clovis G. Chappell; *The Atlantic Monthly* for "The Gift" by Laura Spencer Porter; Dodd, Mead & Company for "Lord of the Far Horizons" by Bliss Carman from *Bliss Carman's Poems,* and for "The Vigil of Joseph" by Elsa Barker; Harper & Brothers for "Childhood" by John Erskine, "Christmas at Babbitt's" by Henry H. Tweedy from *Masterpieces of Religious Verse,* copyright, 1948, by Harper & Brothers; *Good Housekeeping* for "Let Us Keep Christmas" by Grace Noll Crowell; Houghton Mifflin Company for "The Song of a Heathen" by Richard W. Gilder; Virgil Markham for "How the Great Guest Came" by Edwin Markham; Charles Scribner's Sons for "The Spirit of Christmas" by Henry van Dyke, material from *The Spirit of St. Louis* by Charles A. Lindbergh, "O World" by George Santayana; Nancy Byrd Turner for "The Christmas Star."

Preface

$\mathcal{D}$ICK SHEPPARD, beloved minister of the last generation, wrote, "I do love Christmas—to me it is like a Gothic ruin come to life for twenty-four hours." What a grand description of Christmas! Yet, is it not true that Christmas is more like a living cathedral, a thing of beauty, hallowed by time and devotion, and acquiring more splendor with each passing year?

After nearly two thousand years, the old, old story is still strengthened by the great flying buttresses which maintain its stability despite the ravages of time and the alterations of opinion. These buttresses are the faithful witnesses of devout men and women who through the centuries have found at the manger the personality of the eternal God. From Bethlehem still streams a light not of this world and a message of eternal salvation.

In the pages of this book we have returned, as by a journey of faith, to Bethlehem to rediscover and then to recapture, as best our words may, the glory of Christ's

5

nativity. We believe that His story still brings—at Christmas and throughout the year—a divine radiance into the questing hearts of men.

Charles L. Allen
GRACE METHODIST CHURCH
ATLANTA, GEORGIA

Charles L. Wallis
KEUKA COLLEGE CHURCH
KEUKA PARK, N. Y.

Contents

1 ★ Christmas Is a Simple Story

THE CHRISTMAS STORY is serenely simple. It cannot be complicated with philosophizing or with argument; it defies analysis and silences calculation. It is as simple as the silent dawn, as unbelabored as the bursting rose, as unsophisticated as a child's cry, as spontaneous as a child's laughter.

God through the centuries has manifested Himself in diverse and complex ways. We see an evidence of Him in the perfection of a mathematical formula and in the order of a distant galaxy; we hear Him speak through the profound utterances of noble minds and in the erudite thoughts of great theologians. But Christmas is like none of these. Christmas is as simple as childhood and as beautiful.

When God made His most benevolent gesture of fatherly love, His giving of a Son, He wanted to be understood by all men. But no flaming chariot bore Jesus from highest heaven. No mighty cannonade announced His appearing. There were no bugles, no treading of armies, none of the grandeur and glory we should devise for so remarkable an event.

Rather, silently and unobtrusively, Christ entered our world in the way each of us has come, as a weak and helpless child. Why? When surely legions of angels might have heralded His approach, why did God choose from the most obscure of villages the most unpretentious of maidens? Was it not that by sharing our nature, His Son would speak our language, understand our homes, sympathize with our heartaches, comprehend our hopes? Had He come in grandeur, He would have been for us an unapproachable object of wonder and awe. Had He come as a mighty conqueror, we should have honored Him, but we would also have feared Him.

> To be Himself a star most bright
> To bring the wise men to His sight,
> To be Himself a voice most sweet
> To call the shepherds to His feet,
> To be a child—it was His will,
> That folk like us might find Him still.
> —From "Childhood," by John Erskine.

And yet is there in all creation a more miraculous evidence of God's creatorship than a newborn baby? Is there in all the vast reaches of the universe a more wonderful expression of divine love than the child's first cry?

The divine messenger who announced to Mary the word of His coming said, ". . . the power of the Most

High will overshadow you; therefore the child to be born will be called holy, the Son of God" (Luke 1:35).[1] A holiness attends all births, and the promise which every newborn child brings to a mother's heart is an evidence of God's love.

Christ came into the world as a baby. He left the world thirty-three brief years later when He was in the vigor and beauty of noble and consecrated young manhood. From that day to this, there has been no more wonderful expression of God's heart than the promise of childhood and the fulfillment of maturity. All life has become more precious, more consecrated and less expendable because of Him who has shown us the possibilities that lie within our human nature.

Christmas is a simple story, divinely simple yet profoundly inspiring, showing what life may mean for each of us.

[1] All Scripture references, except those otherwise indicated, are from the Revised Standard Version.

2 * The High Road of the Spirit

MANY ROADS LEAD to Bethlehem. Mary and Joseph journeyed from Nazareth along roads crowded by people from many villages, who, at the command of Caesar, were to be enrolled. The wise men crossed the desert waste lands. The shepherds sought new wonders along the familiar home-town byways. But the first road to Bethlehem is unlike all other roads. It is the highway of preparation, spanning time and circumstance. It is the high road of the spirit.

Christmas did not just happen. For centuries men had anticipated Christmas in their hearts, looking forward eagerly to that hour of destiny when in the fullness of time God would reveal Himself in a more wondrous way than ever before.

The road of faith is an ancient road—and at times a dangerous and a narrow one. It was not always crowded nor were there always travelers upon it, yet along it moved men of adventurous spirit and women of the pilgrim heart. These knew it was God's highway and, although they could not discern their destination, they knew that their traveling was in the companionship of the Eternal. So they walked hopefully, expectantly, perhaps recalling the assurance of the psalmist, "Thou dost show me the path of life . . ." (Psalm 16:11).

The need of common men for God led them on. The prophet had promised, "I [God] will lead the blind in a way that they know not, in paths that they have not known I will guide them. I will turn the darkness before them into light, the rough places into level ground . . ." (Isaiah 42:16). Those who were spiritually blind hoped for a day of spiritual vision; those who were despondent or timid awaited a day of light. For surely ". . . the path of the righteous is like the light of dawn, which shines brighter and brighter until full day" (Proverbs 4:18).

Long before Christmas, God prepared His people. How the words of the prophets radiate a faith in the coming of the Wonderful Counsellor and the Prince of Peace! How the lives of men were changed, generation after generation, as men of faith journeyed toward the day of hope! The way of the Lord was built with human sighs and human aspirations and at the end of the road was a manger. From that manger lead all the roads of our lives.

The Divine Roadbuilder is God. If we follow the route He has mapped for our lives, we too will find a glory at our road's end. There may be detours, hazards and delays, but the highway of the Lord leads to the heights of vision and promise.

God guided many faithful persons to Bethlehem. He still leads all who will follow His guidance.

> Lord of the far horizons,
> Give us the eyes to see
> Over the verge of sundown
> The beauty that is to be.
> Give us the skill to fashion
> The task of Thy command,
> Eager to follow the pattern
> We may not understand.
> —From "Lord of the Far Horizons,"
> by Bliss Carman.

3 ★ Journey to Bethlehem

NAZARETH, THE HOME of Mary and Joseph, was nestled in a fold of the hills of lower Galilee from whose heights Joseph could look upon a panorama which extended a score or more miles in three directions. The lowlands teemed with activity; great caravan routes could be seen in the distance. People had left important centers of activity and they moved on toward the great commercial centers which Joseph knew only by hearsay.

Nazareth was not the kind of town about which people boast. "Can anything good come out of Nazareth?" (John 1:46) was no doubt a typical attitude of those who resided in more fortunate locations. But Nazareth was Joseph's home where he had long lived and where, perhaps, when he died he would be laid with his fathers nearby.

Nothing much happens in a town like Nazareth. Yet it was in that unlikely spot that a meek man and a humble young woman inherited the earth, for it was there that the Lord made Himself known to Joseph and to Mary. These common persons had an uncommon faith in God and in His purposes. They believed what the lords of the earth would have doubted. Through them a glory came to Nazareth, and because of them Nazareth has been spoken of with reverence through the centuries.

Because of his great faith, Joseph accepted Mary as only great faith and love can. Anxiously and lovingly he prepared for the birth of her Child. But his best-laid plans for her comfort and convenience were rudely interrupted, for "In those days a decree went out from Caesar Augustus that all the world should be enrolled" (Luke 2:1). Joseph could not expect the arm of Rome to be withdrawn merely because a Jewish maiden was soon to give birth to a child, so he left his home and woodworking shop and journeyed with Mary to Bethlehem that they might register their names on the census rolls.

The wise men traveled from the distant east, but presumably their trip was not without some measure of creature comfort, for they were men of wealth. Joseph was poor and little could he offer to Mary in the way of travel conveniences. No doubt he walked by the side of a small beast of burden upon which Mary rode. The road from Nazareth to Bethlehem was rough and hard, the dusty way probably crowded with many weary travelers, for all Galilee moved toward the city of David.

The road was tediously long, some eighty-five miles' distance. But they did not travel alone for on that road to Bethlehem they were companioned by God and guided by His Spirit. Always the steps of a good man are ordered by the Lord. Always the Lord of highest heaven dwells also with those who have humble and contrite hearts.

At last they came into the City of David, honored in history and rich in legend, but there was none to offer hospitality to them, and the only resting place they could secure was in a stable. The road to Bethlehem did not end in that shadowed stable, for from that humble spot, brightened for a moment by a splendor of Oriental wise men and restive shepherds, there came One who was to become the Guide for the spiritual pilgrimages of millions of the common children of the earth.

4 ★ The Mother God Chose

O F ALL THE women of history, the most honored is Mary, the mother of Jesus. She stands apart from all other women; none is to be compared with her. Mary has been exalted in poetry, fiction and drama; her face is seen on canvas, in bronze, marble and stained glass and we prize the lovely hymns and carols that sing of her. She is enthroned within our own hearts.

No matter what your church or faith, Mary the mother of Jesus is there! Humble and yet divinely serene, her face holds a light that comes from beyond this world. She is beloved as the gentle Jewish maiden to whom God and the angels spoke, not quite understanding all that happened to her and yet of such profound spiritual depth that she gave herself without question to the purposes of God, praising Him in that haunting "Magnificat" for making

17

her "the handmaid of the Lord." She is honored as the noblest of all mothers, the personification of purity, comeliness and submission to God. Through her God became man in Christ, and that is a glory never granted any other woman in all time, upon our earth. She surrendered her life in love to Him, losing herself, that through Him we might be saved. There is, there could be, but one Mary.

True are the words of the angel, ". . . blessed art thou among women" (Luke 1:28, KJ).

Who was Mary? What kind of person was she? What life did she live? It is generally believed that she was directly descended from David. According to ancient tradition, her parents were Joachim and Anna, very devout and holy people. Mary was reared according to the faith of her fathers, and no doubt she was particularly sensitive to the voice and will of God. When the angel told her of God's plans for her life, Mary replied, "Behold I am the handmaid of the Lord; let it be to me according to your word . . ." (Luke 1:38). The literal meaning of the Greek word which we translate as "handmaid" is "a woman slave." Mary was in bondage to God's purposes; His will was her will.

When Mary first appears in the drama of the nativity, she is an obscure peasant girl of, perhaps, eighteen. No doubt her hands were rough and red from housework in a poor home. Today we see her pictured in the most costly garments; at her feet are laid the world's most precious jewels, yet never in her lifetime did she have more than the simplest necessities of life.

In appearance she may have been like many other Jewish maidens of her age. Nothing distinguished her from the others, yet the eternal God chose her from among humanity to be the mother of His Son. The birth of that Son is unmatched among the miracles of all time. We can no more explain His birth than we can explain the origins of the sun, the moon and the stars. When God sent an angel to tell Mary that she should bear a son she was puzzled and apprehensive. "How can this be," she asked, "since I have no husband?" (Luke 1:34). The angel told her of God's will.

At that time Mary was engaged to Joseph. When she discovered that she was with child, Joseph covered her shame with a blanket of love. St. Matthew says that Joseph, being a just man, was unwilling that she be made a public example. We admire Joseph's attitude for he might have been harsh and cruel. When the angel spoke to Joseph of Mary's innocence and said that her child was of God, Joseph understood and believed. When the Child was born, he named Him Jesus, as the angel had directed.

In later years, Jesus came to understand, too. "He said to them, 'You are from below, I am from above; you are of this world, I am not of this world'" (John 8:23).

Mary's life was hard and difficult. Although the angel had said that she, among all women, was highly favored, hers was not the kind of favor that we want from God. A few days before her baby's birth, she was required to take a long, painful journey to Bethlehem. There were nights of sleeping on the ground along the way, days of riding uphill and down on the back of a donkey. Suppose that donkey misstepped and fell! Finally, in Bethlehem, no room was available. Even when new life stirred within her, only a dirty stable and the company of domestic animals were offered to her. There, in the bleak midwinter, she gave birth to the Son of God.

A few hours later another hard journey was required; because of the fears and suspicions of Herod she must flee her homeland. Through the land of the Philistines to Gaza she traveled, and then out across the measureless, hot desert. How she must have longed to be with her own people! Could not God have spared her this added burden? But she did not question God's will. Gently, lovingly, she cared for her precious Baby.

Finally she returned with Joseph to their home—but what a poor home it was, for Joseph's income was obtained from a one-man carpenter shop in an out-of-the-way village. In the words of Jesus we catch glimpses of the only home He ever knew. He recalled how a candle would light the entire house, how clothes were patched and later patches were patched. Into that little, one-room home were later born at least six other children, four boys and two or more girls. Mary was never to know a life of quiet or days of rest.

Joseph is mentioned only once after the story of Jesus' birth, when he took his family to Jerusalem when Jesus was twelve. He may have died soon thereafter, leaving Mary a penniless widow and mother of seven children. Those were years of drudgery and she lived in relative obscurity.

But for the Son of God she made a home, and that is what He needed. History records that France had sixty-nine kings of which number only three were loved by their subjects. Those three were the only kings who had been raised by their mothers, the others being reared by private tutors, governesses, all disinterested persons.

Mary maintained such a home that her Child found mental stimulation, physical well-being and a spiritual atmosphere. "Jesus increased in wisdom and in stature, and in favor with God and man" (Luke 2:52). The patched clothes were kept clean; the simple food was well prepared. We can imagine that Mary read to her children and talked with them about the problems of life, that she prayed with them about the open hearth and went with them to God's House to worship. That was the kind of home God chose for His Son.

The golden thread woven throughout the fabric of Mary's character is her beautiful and sincere humility. Engraved on her heart were the words of the angel, but this did not make her proud or boastful. When the inn-keeper said that his establishment was already over-crowded, she might have said: "I demand the best you have. I am the mother of God." Instead, "Mary kept all these things, pondering them in her heart" (Luke 2:19).

When Jesus was twelve, we read of a misunderstanding between mother and Child. After the experience in the Temple, Jesus said, "How is it that you sought me? Did you not know that I must be in my Father's house?" (Luke 2:49). Mary was bewildered by His words, but she knew the Boy was growing up and breaking away naturally from the disciplines of His family. Sometimes parental love is selfish; sometimes it is jealous. Mary may have felt at times that she was being shut out of His life, but never did she feel mistreated and never did her Son hurt her.

At the wedding in Cana, we see Mary with Jesus. Some biblical scholars surmise that this may have been the wedding of one of Jesus' sisters. After that hour, however, Mary remains discreetly in the background. On one occasion, while Jesus is speaking to the multitudes, ". . . his mother and his brothers came; and standing outside they sent to him and called him" (Mark 3:31). Such was the manner of the mother God chose. She did not dominate; she did not demand. She gave of herself freely, but she was wise enough to know when to cut the apron strings.

Mary never doubted God. She remained loyal through the years. Then came a day when she heard a mob cry, "Crucify him!" She stayed close by. We read, ". . . standing by the cross of Jesus . . . (was) his mother . . ." (John 19:25). As the nails pierced His hands, they pierced her heart. Poor little mother, how hard the path

God gave to her! How strangely the night in Bethlehem
had been transformed. When Jesus, from the cross, saw
His mother, He gently called to His dearest friend, "Behold your mother. . . ." And to Mary He said, "Woman,
behold your son!" (John 19:26, 27). The disciple placed
his arm about Mary and spoke comfortingly to her broken
spirit.

The last glimpse we have of Mary is in the upper room
where she prays with those who believe in Him. Her faith
in God has been vindicated. Victory has dispelled the
clouds.

There is no record of the time or the manner of her
death, and we do not know where she was finally laid to
rest. Perhaps it is as well, for just as her Son continues to
live in our midst, so too does her gentle life continue to
inspire mothers everywhere.

As we remember the mother God chose, dare we not
believe that He may be choosing us for His service? We
do not ask that our way be easy or that we always understand all that happens. We only ask that we be strong to
give our best and to remain ever true, even as Mary was.

5 ★ Joseph, Son of David

LITTLE IS KNOWN about Joseph of Nazareth. He is spoken of briefly in the Gospels of Matthew, Luke and John, but he is mentioned nowhere else in the Scriptures. Matthew calls him a just man.

In a deep sleep he heard the voice of a messenger from the Lord who said to him: "Joseph, son of David, do not fear to take Mary your wife, for that which is conceived in her is of the Holy Spirit; she will bear a son, and you shall call his name Jesus, for he will save his people from their sins." And Joseph ". . . did as the angel of the Lord commanded him . . ." (Matthew 1:20, 21, 24).

Joseph was descended from King David and his family home was Bethlehem. What mighty wonders of old are mirrored in him—but none so wondrous as God's purpose for him at this later hour. He apparently had migrated to Nazareth where he established himself in the trade of carpentry and where in time he was engaged to Mary, a maiden of that community. He was at Mary's side when Jesus was born. Perhaps these words best express Joseph's mind that holy night:

After the Wise Men went, and the strange star
Had faded out, Joseph the father sat
Watching the sleeping Mother and the Babe,
And thinking stern, sweet thoughts the long night
　　through.

"Ah, what am I, that God has chosen me
To bear this blessed burden, to endure
Daily the presence of this loveliness,
To guide this Glory that shall guide the world?

"Brawny these arms to win Him bread, and broad
This bosom to sustain her. But my heart
Quivers in lonely pain before the Beauty
It loves—and serves—and cannot understand!"
　　　—"The Vigil of Joseph," by Elsa Barker.

When the wrath of Herod was kindled against Jesus,
Joseph took Mary and the Child and together they sought
safety in Egypt. Later the three returned to Nazareth, and
the hand of Joseph protected and provided for the growing
Boy. When Jesus was twelve years old, the devout father
journeyed with Mary and Jesus to the Temple in Jerusalem.

Nothing more is given in the Bible by which we may
complete the tapestry of Joseph's life, although tradition
says that he was considerably older than Mary and that
he died during Jesus' childhood. Soon, however, Jesus as-
sumed the responsibility of the household and probably

also followed the carpenter's trade. His family obligations may account for the fact that Jesus delayed His public ministry until the age of thirty.

A few biblical references and a scattered account from tradition are all we can know of Joseph. But are there not some details which our imaginations may add?

Joseph was, first of all, a God-fearing man who was loyal to the God of his fathers and faithful to their religious practices. Jesus, in His formative years, learned from Joseph the great lessons of faith and morality, of love toward man and God, of service and sacrifice.

Everything we know of Joseph suggests that he was a loving and devoted husband. The teachings of Jesus concerning love for family and neighbor reflect His home training and discipline. The highest compliment which we can pay to Joseph is found in Jesus' teaching that men should call God their heavenly Father. Would this image have come from the lips of Jesus if He had not already known the love and care, the protection and concern of an earthly father?

A little boy, who had been cast in the role of Joseph in a Christmas play, complained that he did not have a "speaking part." Joseph had a silent, though very important role in the drama of salvation. Do not "They also serve who only stand and wait"? On the first Christmas Joseph, silent and stalwart, stood at the side of Mary. When God called upon him, he did as the Lord had bidden him.

6 ★ "And there were . . . shepherds . . ."

THE SHEPHERDS OF Bethlehem did not have far to travel. The wise men followed the dusty caravan routes that led from their eastern countries, but the shepherds did not need to travel by day and night along strange and sometimes dangerous roads. Christmas came to them. Christ was born in their home town and to see Him, the shepherds walked along familiar streets.

High above the roads of Bethlehem the shepherds were tending their sheep, a task often dull and monotonous. One night must have seemed the same as a thousand others. Occasionally there would be a stir among the sheep, and the shepherds would move among the flocks to see if there was trouble, returning to the open fire where they would try to keep warm as they again listened to the yarns and tales which herdsmen had told each other for generations. These common shepherds were doing their duty, as they understood it, by protecting their sheep and earning a meager subsistence for their families.

Then into the midst of their routine lives came a glowing, amazing experience. God pierced the shadows of their common task with a light not of this world and with a message for the ages. Angels sang of wonderful good news and the shepherds went in haste to Bethlehem.

Our lives are like that, too. In our daily living unexpected wonders constantly appear. Here we are, doing our duty with what faithfulness we can muster, and then suddenly life glows. The unexpected happens, our lives take on new dimensions. Never again do our days seem quite so plain.

The shepherds did not question that God had actually manifested Himself to them, for they immediately left the mountainside and hurried into the streets they had walked since childhood. An ordinary day had become extraordinary, and now a town they had known so long became more than commonplace, too. Probably in their hearts those shepherds many times had envied those who journeyed from strange, exotic places and had longed for the day when they too might travel to the golden lands beyond the horizon.

But on Christmas Eve no such wanderlust lingered in their minds. God had come to them. Their home town seemed wonderfully alive with a glory they had never seen before.

Two things stand out in the story of the shepherds. First, any day may become a special day if we have the heart to see its wonders. Second, any town will become more than marvelous to the man who seeks for evidences of God's presence along the most familiar byways.

7 ★ "... we have seen his star ..."

At the top of our Christmas trees most of us fix a star, for in the heavens, high over Bethlehem, there was a star.

The star is an especially meaningful symbol for Christmas. Stars speak of other worlds; their radiance comes from afar and they testify to a realm beyond our earth. Christmas has just such a message for each of us. Above our busy lives, high over our varied activities and above our doubts and fears, there is a Spirit that presides and counsels, plans and guides.

Long before science gave to men exact ways of measuring celestial distances, for reckoning time, for finding directions on endless deserts and on vast oceans, men looked to the stars, and a sense of certainty came into their lives.

The stars are constant and dependable; an astronomer can predict with surety their movements, ascertaining what position a particular star maintained a thousand years ago, and foretelling its movements during a thousand years to come. It is good to know that something is certain, something is steadfast. Human beings are fickle. Our steps turn at the slightest whim; our plans are altered by the weakest argument. But God, like the stars He created, is eternal and steadfast, the same yesterday, today and forever. Like the stars in His heavens, God challenges our weakness by His dependability.

The stars are most clearly seen when it is night. When the earth is darkest, they shine with greatest brilliance. Just so, when we are overwhelmed by clouds of despondency and when our lives are shrouded in a night of fear, then we see most clearly the light of God's truth and the brightness of His all-comprehending love. Could the Almighty have chosen a more suitable or appropriate symbol for Christmas than a star?

The wise men were guided by a star. From their homes they traveled in its light. They did not know the way and they were not sure of their destination but they believed the star, for to them the star represented God's guiding hand. On the night of Christ's birth the Bethlehem star was high above the heads of every man. All men could have seen it, but the wise men followed it. In their hearts was a compelling faith that is a prerequisite for all star-led journeys. If we believe in God, He will guide our steps aright. When we trust Him, He will make bright the way ahead. He who stands among us still is ". . . the bright morning star" (Revelation 22:16).

> Stars rise and set, that star shines on:
> Songs fail, but still that music beats
> Through all the ages come and gone,
> In lane and field and city streets.
> And we who catch the Christmas gleam,
> Watching with children on the hill,
> We know, we know it is no dream—
> He stands among us still!
> —From "The Christmas Star,"
> by Nancy Byrd Turner.

8 ★ ". . . there came wise men from the east . . ."

THE CELEBRATION OF Christmas is always given a certain regal glamour by the story of the wise men, who, journeying long days and weary nights across waste land and desert, came at last to Bethlehem to pledge fealty

to the newborn King Jesus. Theirs was the most complicated itinerary of all those who traveled to Bethlehem.
Yet, long as their journey may have been, only a few pen
strokes in a single chapter in Matthew chronicle their experiences. But how colorful is this story, and how much
the wise men add to the drama of Christ's nativity!

They are called wise men because by profession and
study they had mastered both the lore of books and the
wisdom of the heavens; they were philosophers and astrologers. In that day astrologers observed the heavens in order
to determine the will of God. The wise men had long accustomed themselves to look above the world of men for
guidance from the Most High and their behavior was
formed not by the foibles and folly of men but by the
wisdom of God.

I imagine that those "kings of the east" were objects of
ridicule and scorn when they first announced to their
friends that they planned to make a long journey to a
strange land to worship a new king. Many centuries before Noah had been laughed at when, in obedience to
God, he fashioned an ark and prepared for a flood.

There are other thoughts which our imaginations kin-
dle, for biographical information about the wise men is
not available to us. No names are recorded nor do we
know from what countries they journeyed. Legend has,
however, given us some grand and wonderful details.
Legend says that they were kings of eastern monarchies.
This is a reasonable presumption, for they brought royal

gifts to the Child; they paused long enough at Herod's palace to pay their respects to the local ruler after the fashion of visiting potentates; and, finally, they came asking for One who would be King of the Jews, before whom they knelt. There is no particular reason for limiting their number to three; this number was probably based on the fact that three gifts were presented to Christ. An early tradition says that the kings traveled with a vast retinue of which seven thousand men were left beyond the Euphrates and more than a thousand continued on to Jerusalem. An ancient tradition also assigns names to the kings.

> Caspar, Melchior, Balthazar,
> These are they who followed the star.
>
> Myrrh, and incense, gems and gold,
> These are the gifts they brought of old.
>
> These are the precious, wonderful things
> They brought, as befitting three wise kings.
> —From "The Gift," by Laura Spencer Porter.

The gifts are not without a spiritual significance. Melchior offered gold in recognition of the Child's royalty. Gaspar, or Caspar, presented frankincense, symbolic of Christ's divinity. Balthazar laid before the manger a gift of myrrh, emblematic of the Passion of our Lord. Such is the rich embroidery of legend and lore.

The wise men were wise not only because of their learn-

ing but because they were obedient to the heavenly vision.
When God showed them a star, they followed its gleam.
George Santayana was thinking of this kind of wisdom
when he wrote:

> O world, thou choosest not the better part!
> It is not wisdom to be only wise,
> And on the inward vision close the eyes;
> But it is wisdom to believe the heart.
> Columbus found a world, and had no chart
> Save one that faith deciphered in the skies;
> To trust the soul's invincible surmise
> Was all his science and his only art.
> Our knowledge is a torch of smoky pine
> That lights the pathway but one step ahead
> Across a void of mystery and dread.
> Bid, then, the tender light of faith to shine
> By which alone the mortal heart is led
> Unto the thinking of the thought divine.
> —"O World," by George Santayana.

The wise men of old believed because their hearts were
attuned to God. Men are wise today when, kneeling at the
crib of the Child Jesus, they surrender their human wisdom to the influence of the greater wisdom of God.

Not only were the Magi men of wisdom; they were also
men of courage who left their faraway homes to journey
into an unknown adventure. When they had prepared
themselves for travel, they challenged heroically the winds

and the dangers of the desert. Such courage has ever been one of the essential ingredients of Christian discipleship.

To the wisdom and courage of these men must be added faith. First, they trusted God and His guidance. Second, when they found the new King, they knelt to worship and adore. Third, they again depended on God to lead them back to their homes "by another way." From Bethlehem they trekked beyond history. Yet for one hushed moment they entered into the gospel story before passing from history—to remain in the hearts and imaginations of mankind. Their faith remains to stir and to challenge us.

In the birth of Christ is fulfilled all of the wisdom of the ages. The wise men knew that the heavens declared the glory of God. We too are wise when, like them, we look upward and when, having discerned the heavenly sign, we follow where it leads. God often makes known His will to men, but only those who are wise respond to His guidance.

9 ★ His Name Emmanuel

THE MOST PERSISTENT quest of mankind has been for a more perfect knowledge of God. "Oh, that I knew where I might find him!" (Job 23:3) is the longing not only of Job but also of the deepest recesses of the human spirit. Again and again this desire is found in the Psalms. "My soul longs . . . my heart and flesh sing for joy to the living God" (Psalm 84:2). "My soul thirsts for God, for the living God. When shall I come and behold the face of God?" (Psalm 42:2).

When we have passed into some valley of the shadow, when we cling desperately to straws, when all doors close and the night of grief, or sorrow, or despair seems eternally dark—then we hunger and thirst for God. Or when at some moment of achievement we discern more clearly the road ahead or find at last the heights which rise above normal daily living—then too we desire the companionship of the Lord. I doubt if there was ever a man who did not, at one time or another, look anxiously into the heavens or

longingly into the depths of his heart for some reflection
of God. It is proverbial that even the skeptic or agnostic
at the moment of death asks for spiritual consolation.

God has in innumerable ways revealed Himself to those
who have opened their eyes to see His ministrations, or
opened their ears to hear His voice, or opened their hearts
to His Spirit. God has revealed Himself through inspired
spokesmen, through great books and the Book, through a
casual word providently offered by a friend, through an
insight which breaks suddenly and with enlightenment
within our minds. God is revealed supremely for Chris-
tians in and through Jesus Christ.

The message of the Advent season is found in the
words, ". . . his name shall be called Emmanuel (which
means, God with us)" (Matthew 1:23). Jesus said, ". . .
He who has seen me has seen the Father . . ." (John
14:9). What we know of the character and nature of
God we know through His Son; in Him God is with us.
St. Paul affirms this: "For God who said, 'Light shall shine
out of darkness,' has shone within my heart to illuminate
men with the knowledge of God's glory in the face of
Christ" (II Corinthians 3:6, Moffatt).

Christmas brings many joys, but none is greater than
the knowledge that we have in the Babe of Bethlehem a
reflection of God. Joseph Fort Newton once wrote of
Christmas, "For the first time man was glad about God."
What he meant is that through Christ so many anxious
questions have been answered and so many longings have

been fulfilled that fear and doubt have given way to exaltation and gladness. For each of us the gospel of Christ is the good news about God.

10 ★ God's Inexpressible Gift

THIS VERSE SEEMS particularly appropriate at Christmas: "Thanks be to God for his inexpressible gift" (II Corinthians 9:15). Our Christmas tradition of gift-giving stems from the benevolence of God who has given many gifts to His children. We might speak of the world in which we live as a gift from Him. And there are the gifts of loving friends, smiling children, the beauties of the changing seasons, the promise of day and the rest of night, hope in a world filled with despair, the offer of salvation. Most precious is God's gift of Christ and His life, His teaching, His abiding presence in the heart.

Through our exchange of gifts we emulate in a small way the Spirit of God. When our giving is determined by love and sincerity we share the Spirit of God and, I believe, God blesses our gifts.

But Christmas is more than the giving of gifts. It is

the adjusting of all of life to the will of God. A great preacher of an earlier generation, Henry van Dyke, points to the truth of this through a series of questions:

Are you willing to forget what you have done for other people, and to remember what other people have done for you; to ignore what the world owes you, and to think what you owe the world; to put your rights in the background, and your duties in the foreground; to own that probably the only good reason for your existence is not what you are going to get out of life, but what you are going to give to life; to close your book of complaints against the management of the universe, and look around you for a place where you can sow a few seeds of happiness—are you willing to do these things even for a day? Then you can keep Christmas.

A window atop Mount Tom in Massachusetts contains four panes of glass, each of a different color. Through the pane of brown glass one sees a picture of the Berkshire Hills which resembles the beauties of autumn. Winter is suggested by what one sees through the blue glass. The pane of green glass gives to the hills beyond the youthfulness of spring. And a summer sunset is seen when one looks through the pane of red glass. Always, however, the same Berkshire Hills are in view.

So it is with Christmas. One man, greedy for financial gain, thinks of Christmas as a time for exploitation. A sensuous man considers Christmas as a day for indulgence. Another makes Christmas an occasion for getting presents.

But the Christian is reminded that beyond and above all else Christmas is God's inexpressible gift of love, and brotherhood, and good will, and Christ. Reminded of this, his life is attuned to God and made beautiful as he welcomes into his heart the love of God in Christ Jesus.

11 ★ The Wonder of It All

THE CHRISTMAS EXPERIENCE is so overwhelming that our minds cannot comprehend all of it. No one person sees every facet. On the first Christmas the wise men saw a star which the shepherds missed, but the shepherds heard the singing of angels which the wise men did not hear. Mary pondered in her heart thoughts too deep for the shepherds, and Simeon discerned in Christ a religious significance that even Mary did not perceive. No one sees all of Christmas, but if I were to choose any one perspective it would be that of the shepherds.

They were simple men. When, on the hillside, they were frightened by a great heavenly light, an angel calmed their fears and told of a Baby who had been born. They hurried to Bethlehem and worshiped Christ, becoming the first persons on earth to celebrate Christmas. Then we read, "The shepherds returned, glorifying and praising God for all they had heard and seen . . ." (Luke 2:20).

In one way or another nearly all of us celebrate Christmas. What will you get from Christmas? Some will get only a hang-over and a headache. Others will get a load of debts. Some will get only a day free from work and an opportunity to sleep late. But many will experience the thrill of giving loving gifts to dear ones and of reading the notes on greeting cards.

Best of all are the blessings which Christmas brought to the shepherds. Their first blessing was a sense of wonder. Charles A. Lindbergh, during his famous flight across the Atlantic, recorded:

It's hard to be an agnostic up here in the Spirit of St. Louis, aware of the frailty of man's devices, a part of the universe between its earth and stars. If one dies, all this goes on existing in a plan so perfectly balanced, so wonderfully simple, so incredibly complex that it's far beyond our comprehension— worlds and moons revolving; planets orbiting on suns; suns flung with recklessness through space. There's the infinite magnitude of the universe; there's the infinite detail of its matter—the outer star, the inner atom. And man conscious of it all—a worldly audience to what—if not to God.

Christmas gathers up the happy celebrations of many different people: the joy of the sun worshipers in the return of the light and warmth of the sun-god; the fir tree of

pre-Christian German festivities; the yule log from Ice-
land; the mistletoe from pre-Christian England; Santa
Claus, saint of Holland. To these is added the wonder
which the shepherds experienced. Oh, the wonder of Him
who means so much to so many people and adds depth of
joy to so many traditions! The eternal God come to earth
—that is wonderful.

> Welcome! all Wonders in one sight!
>   Eternity shut in a span.
> Summer in winter, day in night,
>   Heaven in earth, and God in man.
> Great little one! whose all-embracing birth
>   Lifts earth to heaven, stoops heav'n to earth!
> —"The Coming Child," by Richard Crashaw.

The shepherds' second blessing was an inner warmth.
They returned to their fields with a song in their hearts.
Isn't it remarkable how Christmas still warms even the
coldest hearts? Despite Caesar's decree, the weary journey
of a peasant couple, the order of Herod that the children
be slaughtered—the impression of the first Christmas is
one of joy and love. Even today the hearts of men beat
more in unison at Christmas than at any other time.

We have become accustomed to the reports of those
operations wherein surgeons ask healthy persons to "lend"
their hearts to patients. The surgeons operate on the idle
heart of one man while life is maintained through the
heart beat of the other, as the blood flows through the

plastic tubes that connect their bodies. What a perfect picture of what the spirit of Christmas does. We lend our hearts to others through understanding, and sympathy, and good will. At Christmas a cold heart is out of place.

Third, the shepherds found someone to worship. They bowed not to a god whom they feared or from whom they should flee, but they knelt at the crib of a God of love. Man's heart seeks a God like that.

E. Stanley Jones tells of a little boy, the son of missionary parents, who was in school in the United States at Christmas. His parents were far away. When a teacher asked the boy what he most wanted for Christmas, the lad looked at a framed picture of his father on his desk and then replied, "I want my father to step out of that frame!" The eternal God stepped from His celestial frame and came close to man at Bethlehem. Now men could know, and reach, and love God.

At Christmas we may find the shepherds' blessings. We too may be caught up in the wonder of it all and find that inner warmth which sets our hearts aglow. We may lift our hearts in adoration and sing, "Glory to God in the highest."

12 ★ Flight by Night

THERE IS AN epilogue to the high drama of the Christmas story. It brings the story of the angel's song, the wise men's visit and the joy of Mary's heart back to the rough realities of the world in which we live. The epilogue is tragic, and perhaps only those who have been ruthlessly uprooted by fear and prejudice in our day can fully appreciate the flight of Joseph, Mary and the Child into Egypt. St. Matthew relates tersely the blunt facts: "Now when they [the wise men] had departed, behold, an angel of the Lord appeared to Joseph in a dream and said, 'Rise, take the child and his mother, and flee to Egypt, and remain there till I tell you; for Herod is about to search for the child, to destroy him.' And he rose and took the child and his mother by night, and departed to Egypt, and remained there until the death of Herod . . ." (Matthew 2:13–15).

Herod, whose life and actions anticipated the cruel despotism of our generation, had sought to obtain from the wise men information about Him who was born to be King of the Jews. The wise men, led by God, returned to their homes without informing Herod. Herod's wrath waxed hot. He ordered the slaying of all children, lest the One among them might some day challenge his authority. But God once more revealed His will to Joseph, and the holy family departed, under the cloak of darkness, for refuge in a foreign land.

It is strange how life so often dashes us from the heights of joy to the lowlands of despair, from the mountain tops of vision to the valleys of sorrow. This was the bewildering experience of the holy family. One night a star stood high above them, but the next night every shadow was potentially dangerous; from behind a rock or a tree might step one of Herod's informers.

But the Lord God, whom Joseph had obeyed all of his life and whom Mary had loved with a constant faithfulness, did not abandon them in their hour of danger. Very often, in the years that followed, Mary told her Child of the ways in which God always attends His children in their great need. That Child's faith in God never was to waver in an hour of trouble when His friends left nor in an hour of trial when He stood alone with God. We naturally trust God when life moves smoothly, when the waters of experience are untroubled, when the wind brushes gently against our cheeks. But trust in God is even more needful when dangers threaten and when calamity falls with a heavy thud upon our lives. Mary and Joseph knew that God was with them in the stable, and they knew too that they were within His encircling love when they followed the rough road of escape to Egypt.

The Herod of the Christmas chronicle is Herod the Great, who fought his way to power with a strong arm and a clever head. He was zealous and fanatic; fear and suspicion were his masters. He was a despot who cajoled his subjects and ultimately persecuted members of his own family. His was the order which put to death his wife Mariamne and two of their sons. History has given him the benevolent title of "Herod the Great" because he was an empire builder, but he passed to his children a legacy of craftiness and passion. His second son, Herod Antipas, was tetrarch when Jesus was crucified.

"But when Herod died . . ." (Matthew 2:19). The words have the dull, cold, impersonal character of rock. How final are the words which mark Herod's passing in the pages of Scripture. It is like a great sigh of relief. It marks the end of a tyrannical rule. The folly of man had spent itself.

Joseph then took his family into Galilee and once again he returned to his Nazareth home. There ". . . the child grew and became strong, filled with wisdom; and the favor of God was upon him" (Luke 2:40).

13 ★ As We Leave Bethlehem

CHRISTMAS HAS COME and gone. Soon the decorations will be carefully packed away until another year. The elusive pine needles will be swept up. The children will be sent back to school. The thank-you notes will be written and the warm and glowing experience will become a memory.

Some people are also likely to put into a deep freezer their cheerfulness and good will. The boss will become as cranky as ever. People will become themselves once more. But it was good to see what a change could be wrought in the minds and hearts of men, even for a day! Yet Christmas need not be limited to only a day. Christmas can become, as it was meant to be, an attitude toward life that will continue during all of the days that follow.

The roads to Bethlehem were roads of hope and trust, of faith and charitableness. Bethlehem is not a dead end; it is rather the place from which we move with greater good will, deeper faith, more permanent peace of mind and heart. Joseph Fort Newton wrote:

47

Christmas is a prophetic day, looking not so much backward as forward. It belongs to an order of life not yet attained, to a religion not yet realized; to a coming, but distant, time which all prophets have foreseen, when men will be ruled by "the angels of our higher nature," and justice will reign, and pity and joy will walk the common ways of life.

The Bible tells us not only of those who went to Bethlehem, but also of those who went away. The shepherds were watching their sheep on the hills round about Bethlehem when in a vision splendid they were told of Christ's birth. They hastened to His manger. Then they returned to their flocks, ". . . glorifying and praising God for all they had heard and seen . . ." (Luke 2:20). Their rejoicing could not be extinguished with the coming of sunrise on the day after Christmas. Their joy was eternal. Around their camp fires they rehearsed again and again the experiences until, I am sure, their lives, their homes, their work radiated with a continuing joyfulness.

The wise men had stopped at Herod's palace on their journey to Bethlehem. He asked them to visit him before they returned, but ". . . being warned in a dream not to return to Herod, they departed to their own country by another way" (Matthew 2:12). And they returned by a different spiritual way; the old way of life was no longer satisfying. They had found in Bethlehem a new and a better way to live.

As we leave Bethlehem, we ought to leave behind old

grudges, old fears, old sorrows. We ought to continue our adventure of life by praising God and by walking on new and better roads. Some time during the winter we shall need the friendly spirit of Christmas. Some time in the spring we shall want the hope of Christmas. Let us not pack up the true spirit of Christmas when we put away the decorations.

14 ★ Some Never Know He Came

WHEN THE ANGELS went away from them into heaven, the shepherds said to one another . . ." (Luke 2:15). What did they say? What do we say on the day after Christmas? For weeks we anticipate Christmas. We buy gifts and cards, we attend parties and we decorate our homes. We sing carols and contribute to special charities and within our hearts is the spirit of good will and cheer. It is a happy time, but soon it is all over—or is it?

Suppose the shepherds had said: "Well, that was a thrilling experience. The choir from heaven and the words of the angel stirred our hearts. But let's get down to earth now. There are the sheep to be watched."

Or, as we might say: "Let's wash the dishes, clean up the house and get back on the job. There are bills to be paid and the things that have been neglected during the past days." What a shocking letdown!

Dr. Clovis G. Chappell has drawn an imaginary word-picture of one of those shepherds, who had been a youth on that first Christmas night and who now has become old. His grandson sits on his knee as he recalls: "A long, long time ago, when I was little more than a boy, I was out on the Judean hills one night with some other shepherds, keeping watch over the flock. And the angel of the Lord came upon us and the glory of the Lord shone round about us. And we were sore afraid. But the angel said, 'Fear not . . . for unto you is born this day in the city of David a Saviour, which is Christ the Lord. . . . You shall find the babe in swaddling clothes, lying in a manger.' "

The old man's lips cease to move, and there is silence. Then the lad turns and looks with wide, puzzled eyes into his grandfather's face and says: "But, granddaddy, is that all? What did you do when you heard the good news? Was what the angel said really true? Was the Christ Child ever really born?"

The old shepherd sadly shakes his white head and answers: "I never knew. I never went to see. Some say that it is all a myth. Others say they found in Him the light of God, the power for life. But for me, I could never be quite sure. I never did go to see."

The supreme tragedy of Christmas is that its real meaning is unknown or completely neglected by so many people. Millions who celebrate and live by a calendar that reckons time by His birth do not know Him.

On Christmas eve they filled the house, some fifty guests
    all told,
  (O little Lord of Christmas, were you left out in the
    cold?)

And ate and sang, played cards and danced till early
    morning light.
  (O little Lord of Christmas, did they think of you
    that night?)

Next morning came the presents on a glittering Christ-
    mas tree.
  (O little Lord of Christmas, was there any gift for
    thee?)

The dinner was a Roman feast, and how those guests
    did eat!
  (O little Lord of Christmas, were you hungry in the
    street?)

Then came some teas, a movie, and at night the last
    revue.

(O little Lord of Christmas, what had these to do
with you?)

By midnight all were tired and cross and tumbled into
bed.
(O little Lord of Christmas, did they think that you
were dead?)

They all woke up with headaches and no joy in work
or play.
(O little Lord of Christmas, did they mark your birth
that day?)

The love, the joy were good, no doubt; the rest a pagan
spree.
(O little Lord of Christmas, let us keep the day with
thee!)

—"Christmas at Babbitt's,"
by Henry Hallam Tweedy.

But there are others who through the study of His
Word and worship in the church He established have
consecrated their lives to His will. Like the shepherds,
they have said, ". . . Let us go over to Bethlehem . . ."
(Luke 2:15).

15 ★ How to Keep Your Christmas Joy

MY FATHER USED to have the most wonderful garden each year, and we always had fresh vegetables in great abundance. Mother, looking ahead to the cold winter days when the garden would be covered by dead leaves, spent many hours canning the beans, tomatoes and other good things. Then in the months that followed she would go to the pantry and take the jars from the shelves. She made it possible for us to have vegetables all year round.

Could we do something like that with the wonderful Christmas spirit? Perhaps we could store up the good feeling we have at Christmas and let a little of it loose in our lives on each of the days that follow. Let us see how it may be possible.

Christmas begins with a Baby. Bishop Arthur J. Moore tells of a group of men who, laboring in the woods of northwest Canada, were away from the sight of good women for many months. When their wives joined them, the men organized a celebration and brought in a band. Among the women who came was one who had brought her baby. When the band started to play, the baby became frightened and started to cry. A rough old woodsman jumped up and shouted, "Stop the band so we can hear the baby cry."

We remember how Herod tried his hardest to kill the baby Jesus by killing nearly all the babies of Bethlehem; but little Jesus had been slipped away. Suppose that Herod had succeeded in his attempt to kill Jesus. No one can measure what a difference in the history of the world that would have made. What a dreary world this would be without the baby Jesus!

As long as babies are born, the world has hope. Consider the year 1809, for example. It was a bleak and dismal time. A ruthless dictator seemed certain to conquer the world and there was almost no hope left in anyone's heart. One morning in February of that year a traveler walked into a country store in the mountains of Kentucky. He asked, "Anything new happen around here lately?" "Nothing ever happens around here," someone replied. "There was a baby born up at the Lincoln cabin last night—that's all." That was one of the most important things that ever happened in this great country of ours.

In that year other babies were born: Charles Darwin and Gladstone, Tennyson and Edgar Allan Poe, Cyrus McCormick and Mendelssohn. You never know what may happen in the world because a baby has been born.

At Christmas our pulses beat more quickly because we know the coming of that Baby has done more to soften the hardness of the world's heart, to bring hope in the midst of the world's despair and to bring joy in the midst of sadness, than any event that has ever taken place since the beginning of time. As we consider Him, our own hearts are softened and our lives are transformed. I wish we might think about that Baby every day of the year; in that way we shall keep our Christmas joy.

The Bible says, "In him was life." We use the word "life" to describe so many things that we become confused concerning what life really is. A policeman tells me that if I ride with him on a single night's patrol, I will learn something about life. I will see drunks, fights and many of the unpleasant things that happen in a large city. "Until you see what I see," he says, "you haven't really seen life." But is that life?

In the cold winter we longingly read the alluring advertisements about Caribbean cruises. We picture ourselves sunning lazily on the deck of a steamer, listening to the romantic melodies of an orchestra. All our cares and problems vanish. "This is life," the advertisements read. But is it?

Death comes to our homes and takes away a dear loved one. Bravely we encourage each other by saying: "We must face up to this. This is life." Is it? A group throws a wild party and shouts, "This is life!" Is it? We look at a famous painting and exclaim, "It has life!" Is that life?

You see, when we say "life" we mean many different things. So, when John said, "In him was life," just what was he talking about? If we might know, then we would surely know a Christmas joy that can be cherished all year round.

The best known and loved of all Christmas stories, excepting only those in the Bible, is *A Christmas Carol*, by Charles Dickens. This story describes more accurately than any other the life that the spirit of Christmas brings. Old Scrooge was a selfish, heartless man. But at Christmastime the air was charged with good cheer. We see it in the friendliness of Bob Cratchit and in the gentleness of Tiny Tim. At last even old Scrooge surrenders to the Christmas spirit; at Christmas, Ebenezer Scrooge found life.

Dr. Hughes Wagner once spoke to a little girl whose parents had separated. "Doesn't your dad ever come to see you?" he asked. "No," she answered. Then her face brightened and she added, "Except at Christmas. Every Christmas he comes." On that one day the little girl had a loving father. I don't know what that father did on other days, but I believe he came nearer to finding real life on Christmas than at any other time.

Alexander Woollcott told a story that came out of the First World War. One Christmas the Americans in the field heard German soldiers singing a familiar carol. The Americans joined in. They met under a flag of truce and on that battlefield they had a Christmas service, treating each other as friends. This was the spirit of Christmas at work. Certainly that day those men more nearly lived than when they were fighting each other.

"In him was life." Wouldn't it be wonderful if we might really live all through the year!

Especially at Christmas I enjoy reading Edwin Markham's story-poem about the coming of Christ. Conrad, the godly old cobbler, one night dreamed that Christ would come to his shop on the following day. Early the next morning Conrad went to the woods to gather green boughs to decorate his shop for the Lord's coming. All morning he waited, but the only visitor was an old man who asked if he might sit down to rest. Conrad saw that his shoes were worn. Before sending the stranger on his way, Conrad put on his feet the best pair in the shop.

Throughout the afternoon he waited for the Lord's coming, but the only person he saw was an old woman who struggled under a heavy load. Out of compassion, he brought her in and gave her some of the food he had prepared for Christ. She went on her way refreshed. Just as the shades of night were falling, a lost child entered his shop. Conrad carried the child home, and then hurried back lest he miss the coming of Christ. But though he waited long and patiently, Christ did not come. Finally, in disappointment, the old cobbler cried:

> "Why is it, Lord, that your feet delay?
> Did You forget that this was the day?"
> Then soft in the silence a Voice he heard:
> "Lift up your heart, for I kept my word.
> Three times I came to your friendly door;
> Three times my shadow was on your floor.
> I was the beggar with bruisèd feet;
> I was the woman you gave to eat;
> I was the child on the homeless street!"
> —From "How the Great Guest Came,"
>   by Edwin Markham.

How can we keep our Christmas joy all the year? Loving service to others is part of the answer.

But to all of this must be added something more. A pastor in the midwest tells of a woman who came to him for healing. She said: "I have had a bad limp, and medical men say there is nothing they can do for me. I wish you would pray for me."

He said that he would pray with her that she might get close to Christ. "Don't pray about anything else," he told her. They prayed several times, but still she limped. One day she told him of a wrong spirit she held in her heart against another person. She felt she should go to that person in the spirit of love, but she hesitated. Yet as she prayed that she might get close to Christ, she felt more and more that she must face up to the wrong spirit in her heart. Finally, she did the right thing, and it was not long before she was walking without a limp.

At Christmastime we long to be close to Christ. We are ashamed of our wrongs, and we are inspired to change. When we do what we should, marvelous power and peace come into our lives, and our troubles seem to vanish. We need to be close to Christ, not only at Christmas, but throughout the year. Then the joy of Christmas will continue in our hearts.

16 ★ Who Is Jesus?

WHO IS JESUS? This question is naturally asked at Christmas. It is a thrilling question, for Jesus is central in all of the joyous festivities that mark His birth; His influence has kept Christmas a living, vital and deeply significant day through all the centuries. The more we know Him the more Christmas becomes an occasion for thanksgiving and adoration. To answer the question we might search through books to learn what others have said about Him. We might read from the vast treasury of poetry and literature, history and philosophy, devotion and theology. In them we should find grand and eloquent testimonies.

But let us rather just think quietly about Him. As we meditate, many pictures of Him come into focus. We see a young mother sitting by a manger in a stable. We hear a baby cry, and the cry sounds like that of all babies.

Then we picture a young man who lives in a small village. He romps with the other children. He goes to school with them. He learns to handle skillfully the tools in His father's little carpenter shop. At the age of thirty, freed now from domestic responsibilities, He walks about the countryside and preaches to those who will listen. Quietly, sometimes dramatically, always lovingly, He interprets the will of God. God is His single concern. He speaks of God's will and of God's way. He urges, persuasively and eloquently, that men must know God and acknowledge their responsibilities to their heavenly Father. The common people hear Him gladly. At times multitudes throng about Him; when people look upon Him, they sense the presence of God. In Him and through Him God becomes very real.

At times He is very lonely though He has a small circle of intimate friends and a wider circle of enthusiastic admirers. The hearts of many are inflamed with a passionate devotion, but many people turn from Him. His demands and the disciplines He requires are too great. Evil men plot His destruction.

One day we see Him tried before an unfair court on untrue charges. One of His closest friends betrays Him; the other friends flee in fear and He stands alone, courageous and faithful to God's will for His life. He is condemned to die and is nailed to a cross between thieves, leaving only the coat He has worn. The soldiers gamble for the possession of it. Through the courtesy of a friend, His body is given a decent burial.

One by one the scenes in His life come before us; it amazes us that we do know so much about Him. We know less about Caesar, who ruled the world at that time, and we know almost nothing about Pilate, the governor. We do not know who was the wealthiest man of that day, nor have we a list of the most socially prominent families.

Although nearly twenty centuries separate Him from us, our thinking about Him strangely influences us. We feel cleaner, happier, and are ashamed of our sins. We love Him, and our love for Him creates in us a love for others. Our fellowship with Him through faith compels us to affirm that never was there one like Him.

Once Jesus asked His disciples, "Who do men say that the Son of man is?" Simon Peter answered, "You are the Christ, the Son of the living God." Jesus then replied, ". . . flesh and blood has not revealed this to you, but my Father who is in heaven" (Matthew 16:13, 16, 17). We may learn about Jesus by reading books, but we learn about Christ through experience. When we know

Him, we realize that He is divine; our minds and hearts embrace this truth.

Because many people know about Jesus and do not know Christ, they argue about who He is. Christian faith in Christ affirms four things about Him. First, Christ's birth was different from that of all others. An angel appeared to a pure young woman and told her that she would give birth to the Son of the Highest. She was puzzled and asked, " 'How can this be, since I have no husband?' And the angel said to her, 'The Holy Spirit will come upon you, and the power of the Most High will overshadow you; therefore the child to be born will be called holy, the Son of God.' " (Luke 1:34, 35). His birth was of God, and He was divine.

Second, during His life on earth, He had supernatural power. The winds and the waves obeyed His voice. He healed every known sickness. With a small boy's lunch He was able to feed a multitude. He forgave sins. He put a song in the hearts of those who were broken in spirit; He gave hope to the discouraged; He offered strength to the weary. Nicodemus said, "Rabbi, we know that you are a teacher come from God; for no one can do these signs that you do, unless God is with him" (John 3:2). The power He imparted to men is still available to those who believe in Him.

Third, His death on the cross is our doorway into eternal life. His cross is an example of sacrifice and a revelation of God's love, but it is much, much more. That

Friday He did something that forever makes different our relationship to God. For the disciples it was "Black Friday"; their leader had been crucified. God, they must surely have felt, had abandoned His own. But later those disciples realized, as St. Paul testified, that ". . . God was in Christ reconciling the World to himself . . ." (II Corinthians 5:19). When men realized that, they saw the cross, not as God's desertion of man, but as His saving power. Then "Black Friday" became "Good Friday."

Fourth, Christ rose from the dead, and His resurrection is our assurance that beyond the grave we, too, shall live. He said, ". . . because I live, you will live also" (John 14:19). Through Christ we learn the power of endless life. So, because of who Christ is, we gladly commit our lives to Him.

No one questions that a man named Jesus once lived in Galilee. Most of us are familiar with the life He lived, and His words are on the lips of multitudes. When we learn of Him, we love Him.

> If Jesus Christ is a man—
>   And only a man—I say
> That of all mankind I cleave to him,
>   And to him will I cleave alway.

As we read of Him, even in the cold type of the printed Gospels, we begin to feel a closeness to Him, and His life exerts a strange power over us. We know that He was more than a man. So we add Christ to Jesus.

Christ means Messiah, God's anointed. Hosts of people affirm:

> If Jesus Christ is a God—
> And the only God—I swear
> I will follow him through heaven and hell,
> The earth, the sea, the air!
> —"The Song of a Heathen, Sojourning in
> Galilee, A.D. 32," by Richard Watson Gilder.

The strongest evidence that Jesus is the Christ, the Son of God come to earth with power to save men, is not found in the story of His life nor in His words. Rather it is found through what He does for men today. Millions of lives have been transformed by His influence, and in them He lives.

> Whatever else be lost among the years,
> Let us keep Christmas still a shining thing:
> Whatever doubts assail us, or what fears,
> Let us hold close one day, remembering
> Its poignant meaning for the hearts of men.
> Let us get back our childlike faith again.
> —"Let Us Keep Christmas,"
> by Grace Noll Crowell.